Humor books available from InterVarsity Press

All God's Children Got Gum in Their Hair by Steve Phelps
Amusing Grace by Ed Koehler
As the Church Turns by Ed Koehler
Attack of the Zit Monster & Other Teenage Terrors by Randy Glasbergen
Church Is Stranger Than Fiction by Mary Chambers
Climbing the Church Walls by Rob Portlock
Families Off the Wall by Rob Portlock
It Came from Beneath the Pew by Rob Suggs
Less Than Entirely Sanctified by Doug Hall
Motherhood Is Stranger Than Fiction by Mary Chambers
Murphy Goes to Church by Steve Dennie and Rob Suggs
Murphy's Laws of Marriage by Steve Dennie and Rob Suggs
Murphy's Laws of Parenting by Steve Dennie and Rob Suggs
Reborn to Be Wild by Doug Hall
Off the Church Wall by Rob Portlock
101 Things to Do With a Dull Church by Martin Wroe and Adrian Reith
The Potluck Hall of Fame by David Dickerson and Mary Chambers
Preacher from the Black Lagoon by Rob Suggs
Way Off the Church Wall by Rob Portlock

MURPHY'S LAWS of MARRIAGE

BY STEVE DENNIE and ROB SUGGS

IVP

InterVarsity Press
Downers Grove, Illinois

InterVarsity Press® is the book-publishing division of InterVarsity Christian Fellowship®, a student movement active on campus at hundreds of universities, colleges and schools of nursing in the United States of America, and a member movement of the International Fellowship of Evangelical Students. For information about local and regional activities, write Public Relations Dept., InterVarsity Christian Fellowship, 6400 Schroeder Rd., P.O. Box 7895, Madison, WI 53707-7895.

Cover illustration: Rob Suggs

ISBN 0-8308-1674-7

Printed in the United States of America ∞

Library of Congress Cataloging-in-Publication Data

Dennie, Steve, 1956-
    Murphy's laws of marriage/Steve Dennie and Rob Suggs.
      p.   cm.
    ISBN 0-8308-1674-7
    1. Marriage—Humor.   I. Suggs, Rob. II. Title.
PN6231.M3D46   1996
818'.5402—dc20   96-4165
                                         CIP

17	16	15	14	13	12	11	10	9	8	7	6	5	4	3	2	1
10	09	08	07	06	05	04	03	02	01	00	99	98	97	96		

Contents

Introduction

Murphy's Law warns us, "If anything can go wrong, it will." In two previous books we showed how Murphy lurks in the shadows of church life and interferes in the task of parenting. Now we want to illuminate Murphy's role in marriage. Whenever a man and woman pledge their lives to each other, promising to accompany each other through life's ups and downs, Murphy tags along, trying to ensure that the downs outnumber the ups.

Murphy infests all areas of marriage. Murphy is there when:

☐ you stand at the altar and mangle your wedding vows.

☐ a simple activity like sleeping finds you kicking, elbowing and toenailing each other all night long.

☐ disagreements over the silliest little things result in days of stony looks.

☐ household appliances break down the day after the warranty expires.

☐ the location of the missing remote control is a matter of the utmost urgency.

The science of Murphology has sprouted thousands of laws, axioms, theories, corollaries, rules and statutes which explain the ways in which Murphy works. It's a substantial body of knowledge. But Murphy's role in marriage hasn't received nearly enough attention, a situation this book hopes to correct.

Steve Dennie & Rob Suggs

1 / Murphy Ties the Knot

The Proposal Proposition

Your fiancée's best friend will always be able to come up with a more inventive marriage proposal.

The Bad Timing Predicament

The chance of meeting your dream spouse increases when you are with a date or a better-looking friend.

The "Just Friends" Scenario

Stage 1: "We're just friends."

Stage 2: "Really, we're just friends."

Stage 3: "I told you—we're *just* friends."

Stage 4: "Look what's on my finger."

Law of Digit Discomfort

Your fingers will intertwine in the way
most uncomfortable to both of you,
but neither will want to say anything.

The Perfect Couple Rule

The "match made in heaven" will ignite the biggest forest fire.

The Crackerjack Ring Scenario

The more expensive the engagement ring, the more likely you'll break up.

The Real Life Principle

The most serious incompatibilities can be recognized only after the wedding.

The Nuptials Curse

Murphy loves weddings.

Corollary:
The more details, the better.

First Law of Weddings

The more candles, the greater the chance somebody will faint.

Second Law of Weddings

Little kids never walk in a straight line.

Third Law of Weddings: Cards and gifts will get switched, resulting in thank-you notes to people for gifts they never gave.

Inevitable Disagreements Not Covered in Premarital Counseling

1. Which side of the sink (if any) to put the dirty dishes in.

2. How to load the dishwasher.

3. What shelves to put things on in the refrigerator.

4. How many times to hit the snooze alarm before getting up. ⇨

5. Which cupboard holds the glasses.

6. How close to E you can get before filling the gas tank.

7. Where to put the litterbox.

8. Who sleeps on what side of the bed.

9. When, in relation to the expiration date, milk must be dumped.

10. The correct setting for the electric blanket.

11. Whether to sleep with the closet door open or closed.

12. Which drawer to put the silverware in.

The Scapegoat Clause

The guarantee on premarital advice expires on the wedding day.

The Test Score Fallibility

Never believe the results of a compatibility test.

Corollary:
Compatible personalities aren't.

2 / Murphy for Two

The Law of Shared Responsibility

No matter how carefully you divide household chores, the wife's share will always end up being larger.

The Adhesive Aggravation

The more expensive the kitchen utensil, the less chance you'll be able to scrape off the price sticker.

The Noncooker's Law

It's always pizza night.

The Necessity-Is-the-Mother-of-Dishwashing Rule

The pan you need is in the dishwasher, still dirty.

Corollary:
You're out of detergent.

Extension:
Actually, you have another box of Cascade out in the garage, but you won't remember until tomorrow.

Recipe Rules

Recipe instructions use measurement units incomprehensible to men.

The last step in the recipe contains the one ingredient you forgot to buy.

The ingredient you forget to add will be the one whose absence is most noticeable.

Steve's Rule for Food Preparation: If it takes more than two steps, it's too complicated.
Corollary: "Turn on the oven" and "remove the cellophane" each count as steps.

The Mailbag Phenomenon

Even though your spouse is holding ten unopened letters in her hand, she will look over your shoulder to read what's in the envelope you opened.

The Gazette Curiosity

Your spouse's newspaper section always seems more interesting.

3 / Murphy Has a Mortgage

Homebuyer's Rule of Thumb

After carefully listing all possible costs of buying a new home, add another fifty percent.

The Party Illusion

The grand social gatherings you envision, and which determine the house you buy, will occur only once every three years.

Laws of Homebuying

Your counteroffer will be several thousand dollars higher than they would have settled for.

The inspector will discover minor problems while overlooking major defects.

After spending a day touring ten houses, you will make an offer on the first one.

Corollary:
Somebody else will have just made an offer.

The Law of Lawncare Gadgetry

Yard tools accumulate to consume all available garage space.

Corollary:
A two-car garage will hold only one car.

The Law of Lawncare Envy

The grass is always greener in the neighbor's yard.

Corollary:
And it's always longer in your yard.

The Universal Diagnosis

It's broke, and it's gonna stay broke.

Corollary:
Don't try to fix it. Just buy a new one.

Extension:
The more it costs to fix, the less chance it will stay fixed.

4 / The Domestic Murphy

Law of the Shower

The early bird gets all the hot water.

The Law of Makeup Application

The longer you take getting ready, the less chance your husband will compliment you on how you look.

Man's Law of Towel Replacement

If the bath towel is dry, it's clean.

Corollary:
A single guy can use the same bath towel for years without washing it.

Corollary:
A married guy will try.

The Cleanliness Comparison

A woman can shower, wash and dry her hair, and shave her legs in the time it takes her husband to adjust the showerhead.

Corollary:
A semibald man takes more time washing his hair than his long-haired wife.

The Scrub-a-Dub-Dub Discrepancy

The body parts which least need to be cleaned get scrubbed the most.

Corollary:
The soles of your feet never get cleaned.

Snooze Alarm Laws

Early to bed, early to hit the snooze alarm.

If you can get up with the alarm clock's first ring, you will choose a spouse who doesn't become fully conscious until after hitting the snooze alarm every ten minutes for an hour.

Setting the alarm fifteen minutes earlier won't make a bit of difference.

The First Law of the Messy House: Dirty floors attract visitors.

The Second Law of the Messy House

The house gets cleaned only right before visitors come.

The Third Law of the Messy House

Dirty dishes accumulate to consume all available counter space.

The Fourth Law of the Messy House

Husbands and wives use different definitions for *clean.*

The Fifth Law of the Messy House

An unexpected knock on the door causes couples to leap from their chairs, turn off the TV and frantically tidy up the house.

Corollary:
You'll pick up everything before they walk in—except for that one piece of dirty underwear.

Laws of the Laundry Room

No matter how you combine clothes in the washing machine, your spouse thinks it's wrong.

The way your mother taught you to wash clothes will be declared incompatible with your spouse's choice of detergent.

Foolproof Corollary:
Just stay out of the laundry room.

The Garage Sale Conflict

Whatever you throw away, your spouse wanted to keep.

Corollary:
Your trash is your spouse's treasure.

The Propane Law

The grill's gas tank will run out in the middle of doing twenty hamburgers.

The Mystical Load Order Law

Never fill the dishwasher while your spouse is watching. You won't do it right.

The Law of Household Chores: A woman's work is never done.
A man's work will get done . . . but not right now.

The Computer Buyer's Conundrum

If you use a Macintosh at work, she uses Windows.

Corollary:
Buying software for home to match what you use at work causes your employer to switch to a different software package.

Corollary:
If you both use the same computer and software at work, the school system will use something completely different.

5 / The Murphy-in-Law

Behavior Modification Principle

The kids are always better behaved at your sister-in-law's house.

The Wisdom Disparity

Marriage advice given by your mother will work only on your father.

The Dishes Determinate

The chance of your in-laws making a surprise visit is directly proportional to the amount of dirty dishes.

The Learning Curve

In-laws never live up to the stereotypes at first, but given time, they learn.

The Second Guess Rule

Your spouse always knows a better way to do it.

Corollary:
Your in-laws know several better ways to do it.

Extension:
None of which will work.

6 / Murphy Hunts & Gathers

The Wandering Syndrome

The *one time* you don't ask for directions, you'll get lost.

Corollary:
Real men don't ask for directions.

Extension:
Wives of real men are often lost.

First Law of Tool Acquisition

Every household task requires the purchase of a new power tool.

Corollary:
You can always build a case for buying a new cordless drill.

Second Law of Tool Acquisition

The length of the rationale for buying that new power tool is inversely proportional to your need for it.

Third Law of Tool Acquisition

The more expensive the tool, the less you'll use it.

Fourth Law of Tool Acquisition

"Having" is more important than "using."

Fifth Law of Tool Acquisition

There will always be a bigger socket set.

Corollary:
And you really, really need it.

Sixth Law of Tool Acquisition

You can never have too many screwdrivers.

The Mechanic Imitation Rule

Many know how to pop open the car hood and frown when there's a problem. Few have any idea what to look for.

Corollary:
The one who can fix your car is not your spouse.

Extension:
Those who can't fix cars marry others who can't fix cars.

The Law of Curdle Acceleration

You *will* put the milk back in the refrigerator. Just not right away.

Corollary:
Maybe not for several days.

The Blackout Principle

Buried cables are never where they're supposed to be.

Corollary:
You learn this only after knocking out the power for your entire housing development.

Rules for Weekend Handymen

No matter how you measure it, it won't fit.

The Assembly Required Delusion

Affordable furniture which can't possibly be assembled wrong will be.

The Man's Man Solution

If it doesn't fit, use a bigger hammer.

Corollary:
If it doesn't stay together, use duct tape.

7 / Murphy Throws Dishes

The Don't-Let-the-Sun-Go-Down Rule
The sun always goes down ten minutes after wrath occurs.

The Law of Perpetual Placation

Love means having to say you're sorry more than you can imagine.

The Rule for Sensitive Guys

If you think something needs to be made right, it doesn't.

Corollary:
Unless you do nothing, in which case it did need to be made right.

Extension:
The longer you wait, the harder it will be to make it right.

The Silver Lining Reversal

Lurking within the sincerest apology is a criticism visible only to the apologee.

The "Honey, We Need to Talk" Rule

The problem you begin discussing and the solution you reach are never related.

Corollary:
If you begin discussing finances, you'll end up talking about last year's Christmas gathering with your parents.

Bedtime Battles

If you like to read before going to sleep, she doesn't.

Corollary:
And she can't go to sleep with any lights on.

Extension:
Or music.

Laws of the Little Things

If you like buttered popcorn, she has high cholesterol.

If you like to sit on the side of the theater, he likes the middle.

If you like mushrooms, she doesn't.

If you prefer pepperoni, he prefers ham.

If you like Letterman, she likes Leno.

If you suggest Domino's, he'll suggest Little Caesar's.

If you like fragrances, she's allergic to them.

8 / The Romantic Murphy

The Romance Illusion

Taking a shower together means one of you gets a shower and the other gets cold.

The Law of Mood Alignment

When she feels romantic, he wants to watch TV.

When he feels romantic, she wants to read.

When you both feel romantic, the in-laws call.

Corollary:
And they're in a very talkative mood.

The Beauty Salon Effect: No romantic moment is so perfect that it can't be ruined by the smell of a new perm.

The Bedside Rule

If you prefer sleeping on the left side of the bed, so does she.

Corollary:
This is not necessarily a bad thing.

The Active Abstraction

If you're a morning person, he's a night person.

The Law of Intertwined Limbs: As soon as you get comfortable, your spouse will shift positions.

Man's Rule of Foot Care

A big toenail shouldn't be cut until—well, it just shouldn't be cut.

Corollary:
The longer his toenails, the greater the chance they will become embedded in your ankle.

Floral Principle

When in doubt, send roses.

Corollary:
Actions speak louder than words, but roses speak louder than actions.

The Law of Floral One-Upmanship

The day you send roses to your wife at the office, the same florist will deliver a bigger bouquet to one of her coworkers.

The Floral One-Upmanship Alternative

The day you send roses to your wife at the office, she'll have gone home sick.

The PDA (Public Display of Affection) Principle

The more affectionate they appear in public, the less affectionate they are at home.

The Cozy Deception

If they're sitting on the same side of the booth, they don't have anything to talk about.

The Candlelight Mood-breaker

The more romantic the restaurant's atmosphere, the greater the chance two crying children will be seated at the next table.

9 / TeleMurphy

The Salesperson Indication

If they call you "Mr." or "Mrs.", they're selling something you don't need.

Rules of the Telephone

You can never remember the autodial presets.

The message on the answering machine isn't for you.

The more important the phone message, the greater the chance your spouse will forget to tell you about it.

The phone will ring when you're both in the bathroom.

Corollary:
If you try to get to the phone, you'll be one ring late.

Laws of the Remote

The remote is always lost.

Remotes attract other remotes.

Men believe that the remote control is God's way of compensating them for the missing rib.

Even when the TV isn't on, the man likes to hold the remote.

The Law of the Prodigal Remote

To find a missing remote, turn on the TV manually, then sit on all of the cushions in the room until you hear the volume rising to an unbearable pitch. It's under that cushion.

Rule of Contrived Submission

Let him have the remote. It'll make him think he's in charge.

The Channel Surfing Dictum

As soon as you get interested in a show, your husband will flip the remote.

Corollary:
The wife never has more than ten seconds to get interested in a show. Then it's gone.

The Rule of VCR Impairment

The more important the TV show, the less likely you'll program the VCR correctly.

Corollary:
No TV show is important.

The TV Incompatibility Rule

The fewer the channels, the more likely you'll disagree about what to watch.

Extension:
If it interests you, it won't interest your spouse.

Corollary:
You'll mostly watch shows that don't particularly interest either of you.

The Parallel Lives Principle

Husbands and wives watch, but don't *see*, the same movie.

Cable Subscriber's Observations

There are never enough channels.

The more channels you have, the less chance you'll find something that interests you.

The more channels you have, the fewer channels you'll actually watch.

Cable subscribers keep the TV on the same channel.

Corollary:
While doing things in other rooms.

The Super Bowl Law: The more important the sports event, the greater the need to spend the time doing something with your spouse.

Corollary: You always need to spend more time with your spouse.

10 / Murphy Goes for Broke

The Law of Redundant Coverage

Multiple insurance policies overlap so as to minimize the reimbursement for any particular medical need.

The Simple Answer

Whatever you did—it's not covered.

The Killjoy Principle: Every inheritance windfall is met with an equal-size unexpected medical bill.

The Law of Shrinking Returns

Bills accumulate to consume all discretionary income.

Corollary:
Then you have children.

Extension:
One minute into the new year.

The Housecall Principle

There is always an easy solution, known only to a highly paid service person.

Law of Appliance Decay

The more expensive the service contract, the less chance the appliance will need repairs.

Corollary:
If you don't renew the service agreement, it will break down.

Extension:
At the worst possible time.

Further Extension:
Like on Thanksgiving Day while the turkey is cooking.

Shopping Laws

Every calendar event requires buying a new article of clothing.

Every new dress bought on sale requires a new set of earrings at full price.

Today's purchase is tomorrow's sale item.

The discount on any item is a more important consideration than the cost of the item.

Corollary:
Or the need for it.

The Featuritis Principle

The more new features it has, the easier it is to rationalize it to your wife.

Corollary:
Or so she lets you think.

The Plastic Assumption

Affordable equals breakable.

Corollary:
The more affordable, the more breakable.

11 / Murphy Can Relate

The Law of Error Detection
Any factual misstatement is immediately recognized by your spouse.

Corollary:
And pointed out to you before you can correct it.

Extension:
Preferably in public.

The Attention Deficit Directive

An ounce of listening is worth a ton of "I told you so."

The Law of Inverted Perceptions

If you see it as a molehill, your spouse sees it as a mountain.

The Hot Tub Principle

You never really know when you're in hot water.

Corollary:
You can't get out of hot water; you can only let it cool off.

The Fess-Up Principle

The sooner you confess, the better.

Corollary:
Your spouse knows anyway.

Three Stages of the Doubting Spouse

1. "Honey, your idea won't work."
2. "Honey, your idea might work, but it's not worth the effort."
3. "See, honey—I knew it would work."

The Hairdo Expectation

The more subtle the hairstyle change, the greater her expectation that you notice.

Corollary:
The new hairdo isn't.

Extension:
It *was* a week ago, when you *should* have noticed.

The Law of Intuition Refutation

Never admit that your wife correctly guessed what you were thinking just now.

Women's intuition always vetoes the facts.

If the facts don't fit your intuition, they must be discarded.

Law of Spousal Irritants

The amount of annoyance is inversely proportional to the subject's importance.

Corollary:
The more minor the irritant, the greater the irritation.

The "What Did He Have to Say?" Response

A husband can summarize, in about ten words, a thirty-minute phone conversation.

Corollary:
That's a lengthy explanation.

The Law of Few Words

The more something's bothering him, the less chance he'll talk about it.

12 / Murphy's Night Out

The Law of the Uneventful Weekend

Only other couples do interesting things over the weekend.

The First "Are You Going to Wear That?" Law

No matter what combination of clothes you put on, your spouse says something doesn't look right.

The Second "Are You Going to Wear That?" Law

No matter what jacket you select, your spouse will think you'll get either too cold or too hot.

The Boring Couple Routine

"We went out last night" means you spent an hour eating at Bob's Big Boy, then went home and spent the rest of the night watching sitcoms.

The Fantasy Getaway Observation

You're not going anywhere.

The Early Warning Rule

Your spouse will remind you to turn left two seconds before you would have hit the turn signal on your own.

The "Let's Go Back and Check" Rule

If you're not sure you turned off the oven, you did.

The 100 Mile Statement

I thought *you* locked it.

The R & R Delusion

Relaxing vacations aren't.

The Pit Stop Rule

When you see him grab a book and head in the direction of the bathroom, you're not going anywhere soon.

13 / In Murphy & in Health

Laws of Conflicting Schedules

Your company Christmas party will occur on the same night as your spouse's.

If you both have a meeting at church the same night, they will begin at different times.

The Law of Snapshot Obsolescence

By the time you arrange the photos in a scrapbook, you can't remember when or where the photo was taken.

Corollary:
You may not even recognize the people.

The Fat Forecast

The largest part of the closet is the "when I lose weight" side.

The First Law of Exercise

There is always an excuse *not* to exercise.

The Second Law of Exercise

The more exercise equipment you buy, the more weight you'll gain.

The Third Law of Exercise

The expensive exercise machine you bought will be at your neighbor's garage sale for a tenth of the price.

The Fourth Law of Exercise

The expensive exercise machine you bought which takes up a lot of space and never gets used will be at your garage sale the following year.

The Illness Error

The statement "I'm not contagious" is always false.

The Spreading Situation

When you are sick, your spouse will be sick.

Corollary:
Kids too.

The Procrastinator's Rationale

Procrastination gives purpose to life: You always have something important to do.

The Procrastinator's Escape Clause

Never put off today what you can tell your kids to do.

Corollary:
Telling your spouse to do it is the same as putting it off.

Law of the Gene Pool: Bad habits are hereditary—your children get them from your spouse.

The Wimp Factor

One spouse's minor headache is the partner's incapacitating neural trauma.

Corollary:
Aspirin can remove a headache, but wimpiness has no cure.

The Wimp's Pain and Suffering Opportunity

Any headache, back pain, simple bruise or flulike symptom is grounds for pampering.